Tips and W

Wrinkle (definit
A piece of servic
Concise Oxford Dictionary

edited by Mary Sansbury and Anne Fowler
illustrations by Anne Fowler

tips and wrinkles

a treasury of household hints to save time, energy
and money around the home

Pan Books London and Sydney

First published 1972 and sold in aid of Bristol local charities
This revised edition published 1978 by Pan Books Ltd,
Cavaye Place, London SW10 9PG
© Mary Sansbury 1972, 1977
ISBN 0 330 25212 7
Printed and bound in Great Britain by
Richard Clay (The Chaucer Press) Ltd, Bungay, Suffolk

contents

ACKNOWLEDGEMENTS We would like to acknowledge with very grateful thanks all the ingenious ideas we have received from the members of St Oswald's Fellowship, St Albans Church, Bristol, and the readers of *Woman's Own*, and are only sorry that we have been unable to include all of them.

We would also like to thank *Woman's Own* and all those who have kindly helped with the original typing and editing.

Mary Sansbury, Anne Fowler

Royalties from this book will be divided between the Age Action Trust incorporating the British Foundation for Age Research, and charities for the elderly in Bristol.

around the house

Make friends with your clothes pegs! Use them for numerous other little jobs – securing open grocery packets, closing a polythene bag containing food in the fridge, clipping together shopping lists or other papers at your desk.

Extra airing space can be obtained by stretching plastic spring wire across the back of the airing cupboard door and also across the door frame.

If your *zip fastener* does not run freely, rub the teeth with a lead pencil.

Cut a piece of foam plastic to fit the base of an *umbrella stand* to soak up the drips.

To avoid drips when *pouring wine*, finish with a slight rolling action and a slight upward jerk of the bottle.

Excellent *pipe cleaners* may be made from good strong feathers, e.g. those from crows, rooks, pigeons.

Television glare ? Try wearing sunglasses.

A paperclip by the central fold will prevent a *newspaper falling apart*.

Place a small button at the end of your *sellotape roll* ; the end will be easier to find and the button easily removed.

To loosen *sellotape that has become stuck,* heat over steam for a couple of seconds and it will come away immediately.

A quick way to *clean venetian blinds* – wear an old pair of fabric gloves, dip fingers in warm soapy water and then draw each slat between the fingers.

Rub furniture polish on a metal *curtain track* to prevent rust and promote smooth running.

Talcum powder applied to *curtain rails* assists drawing and opening curtains, particularly if the rails are slightly rusty.

Drawings curtains at dusk during winter helps to keep rooms warm.

Window cleaning. Alternative aids are :
1 A little vinegar in plain warm water.
2 Methylated spirits.
3 Old newspaper crumpled into a ball and slightly damped. This is both effective and economical.

Polish off with dry newspaper.

When there are more than one pair of *curtains* at a window, number them and change the order at intervals to spread the fading hazards.

If a *casement-type window has stuck*, place a small flat piece of wood on the hinged frame where it is tight and hammer on this to free the window. This saves damage to the paintwork.

To prevent *slipping mats* :
1 Glue on pieces of foam rubber, or
2 Sew on jampot washers, or
3 Apply big dabs of Copydex.

These are all best applied under the corners of the mats.

Empty plastic Vim containers are very handy when a *sprinkler* is needed, for any scouring or detergent powder. The tops are easily prised off for filling and clipped back again. Make sure to label the contents !

Pop a polythene bag over the head of your *squeezy sponge mop* after use to prevent it drying out and cracking. This will add months to the life of the sponge.

Make your own *funnel* from the top of a plastic detergent bottle. Cut through it about 10 cm (4 inches) from the top and invert to use as a funnel.

Legs of nylon stockings are useful for *straining* purposes, instead of muslin.

Place *messages for tradesman* in a plastic bag and secure with a clothes peg – and the rain won't matter.

Use rubber gloves, or a damp sponge or foam rubber, *to pick up cotton etc, from carpets* or upholstery.

Make rubber gloves last twice as long! When new turn them inside out and stick a strip of sticking plaster across the top of each finger. This is especially effective if you like to keep your nails long.

Before throwing away worn rubber gloves, cut strips from the cuffs which will make some strong and *useful elastic bands*.

Cigarette ash rubbed with your finger will *remove wax crayon* from any smooth surface.

To prevent pictures or mirrors making marks on the wall, stick corn plasters at the back of the corners.

A raw lemon rubbed on the *ivory handles of knives* or on piano keys will help to remove yellowing.

Cooking foil makes an attractive cover *to protect your precious dining table* for a children's party.

Cottonwool buds can be used for all sorts of jobs, including cleaning narrow teapot and coffee-pot spouts, and crevices behind the bathroom taps.

Furniture polishes
1 Mix an eggcup each of paraffin oil and vinegar in a screw-top jar. Put in a duster to absorb the liquid, then hang it out to dry. Keep in the jar or a plastic bag. It will absorb dust and preserve the furniture.
2 Equal quantities of linseed oil and vinegar may be used in the same way.

White *stains on highly polished furniture* may be removed by using several different materials.
1 Camphorated oil.
2 A Brazil nut (rub with the cut surface).
3 Brasso.

4 Cigarette ash mixed with olive oil into a paste.
   Rub round gently, leave to dry and polish in
   the usual way.

Cleaning copper. Old and badly stained copper
can be immersed for a few minutes only in a
solution of Harpic in water. When the copper
begins to turn colour remove it and rinse
thoroughly. Finish polishing in the usual manner.

Salt and vinegar, or half a lemon dipped in salt,
are also good ways of *cleaning copper*. Clean off
quickly and rinse well before the final polishing.

Lemon juice mixed with Brasso will help to
brighten brass and keep it clean longer.

When *cleaning neglected brass*, the polishing will
be made easier if you clean the brass first with a
solution of strong ammonia.

bedroom and bathroom

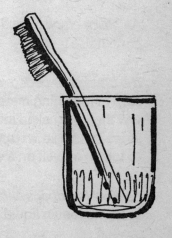

Nail polish. Always unscrew and rescrew top of bottle when dusting dressing table; this prevents it sticking.

Add a few drops of nail polish remover to *thin, hard or tacky nail polish*. Shake the bottle and you're all set to go. Remember to allow extra time for it to dry.

To clean a diamond, use a drop of whisky or gin.

Polish jewellery with toothpaste, or tooth powder, on an old toothbrush.

Keep spare tablets of *scented soap* among your handkerchiefs.

An alarm clock placed on a tin plate makes a lot more noise!

If a blanket or bedcover is too short, sew a wide strip of matching material to the bottom which will then be tucked in and not seen. Similarly, strips can be sewn to the sides of an eiderdown to tuck it in well on a child's bed.

Leather handbags and suitcases can be cleaned with Meltonian liquid wax or cream.

A Youth Hostel-type fine *cotton sleeping bag* takes no room to pack and will save your hostess's sheets for the odd, casual overnight stay.

An old spectacle case makes a useful container for scissors, needles, thread, etc, when travelling.

An empty lipstick case makes a handy container for *hairgrips*.

Dig out the remains of your *used lipstick* with a matchstick, shape into a sausage shape, and harden in deep-freeze or ice-box for further use.

A newly-ironed garment will crease again very quickly, so avoid wearing or packing it until several hours later.

When packing clothes, fold them over rolled-up plastic bags instead of tissue paper, as these stay more 'springy' and so help to prevent creases being formed.

When folding garments, make the folds crosswise and not lengthwise where possible. The creases will then drop out more easily when the garment is unpacked and hung up.

To pack coat-hangers tidily, first take out hooks and pack them separately in a bag.

Sew large tape loops, at waist level, to the inside of each side seam of *your long evening dress*. Turn the bodice out over the skirt and hang the loops over the coat-hanger. This way the dress will hang well above the floor of your wardrobe, free from dust.

To 'iron' a handkerchief in an emergency, ease it out flat while still wet on a mirror or on the glass of a picture and leave until dry.

Canvas shoes are invaluable for *walking on holiday* in hot, dusty countries, where sand and grit are a hazard with sandals.

To dry out the insides of wet shoes or boots, stuff with newspaper.

A hand hairdryer is very useful for *drying out the insides of wet wellington boots*.

To renovate black clothing, rub with a rag soaked in turpentine which will help to remove shininess.

Hang *navy or black skirts* inside out to guard against dust and fluff

A piece of sellotape wrapped round your finger sticky side out will *collect hair, fluff, etc from dark material*.

Ordinary *cotton or surgery wool will go twice as far* if you unfold it carefully and put it in an airing cupboard or on a radiator. It will swell to twice its size.

A £1 note in a sealed envelope as a reserve in an emergency is a very useful addition to your handbag.

Tights with a ladder in one leg can still be used if you have two of a matching colour. Cut off the laddered legs and discard them. Then adjust the remaining portions so that one has a right leg and one a left and wear both at once.

If you enjoy *reading in the bath*, first warm your spectacles and they will then not steam up.

When filling a hot water bottle for the first time, put a few drops of glycerine into the water ; this will make the rubber more supple.

Face flannels which become slimy due to an accumulation of soap can be boiled in a weak solution of vinegar (one teaspoonful per pint of water) for ten minutes. Rinse in water to which you have added a few drops of ammonia, and then give a final rinse in clear water. As a preventative, put flannels in washing machine weekly.

To revitalize a slimy natural sponge, soak it overnight in a bowl of warm water and dissolved soda crystals. Next day wash through with warm soapy water (it still *feels* slightly slimy at this stage) and leave until thoroughly dry. It is then ready for action again.

For cleaning baths and basins, use liquid or powdered detergent, as it is much better for the enamel surface than the proprietary abrasive powders.

To remove coppery green and tan stains in the bath, cut a lemon and smear the juice (citric acid) on the offending areas. Leave for a couple of minutes and wash off thoroughly.

Press silver paper or kitchen foil to the dampened underside of your *soap*. It will last longer and be far less messy.

To reconstitute small pieces of soap into a tablet, put them into an old cup with a few drops of glycerine and steam in boiling water until the mixture softens. When cool, press into a ball, then shape it with your hands into a tablet.

Sew together two pieces of foam sponge (about 15 cm or 6 inches square), leaving a small opening along one side, and pop in all those small leftover bits of soap. It makes *an excellent soap sponge* for the children's bathtime.

Don't throw away *that old loofah*. Cut it into pieces and use it with detergent for cleaning paintwork, worktops, sinks and baths — and it will not scratch non-stick pans.

A little mild detergent added to the *bath water* prevents a dirty ring forming round the bath. (Bubble bath liquids have the same effect — at greater cost!)

To crush a medicinal tablet, place between two teaspoons fitted together with their handles out on opposite sides and apply grinding pressure with a thumb in the bowl of the upper spoon.

An ice-cube placed on the tongue will temporarily numb the taste buds and make it easier *to swallow really unpleasant medicine*. Similarly, ice will numb the skin before taking out a splinter.

To clean dentures, brush hard with dry bicarbonate of soda as an alternative to denture powder, and rinse well.

To avoid blisters for walking holidays, charity

walks and the like, treat the feet for at least a week previously by rubbing night and morning with surgical spirit. Allow to dry and dust lightly with talcum powder. When walking, wear two thin pairs of socks (preferably not nylon) and shake a little talcum powder into each sock and into the shoes.

Shabby patches on shoes may be touched up with children's Airfix gloss paint. Many colours are available.

A paper bag kept in your wastepaper basket is handy for disposing of used paper hankies — especially if you have a cold. 'Trap those germs!'

If you really cannot get to sleep (and have counted all the sheep!) find a really dull book, or try reading your dictionary.

Disturbed sleep due to traffic or a noisy hotel may sometimes be overcome by the use of earplugs.

Make-up tips
Use cotton wool instead of *a powder puff* and change it frequently.

Loose face powder is more economical for use

at home: brush off excess, then a pad of damp cotton wool squeezed out well and pressed all over the finished make-up will 'fix' it through the day.

A simple face mask Clean your face in the normal way, then smear a little raw egg white over it. Leave for fifteen minutes (longer for oily skin) then rinse with tepid water. You can feel it drawing the impurities out of your skin. Do this once a week for a clearer complexion.

To help dandruff, mix equal parts of vinegar and water, part hair all over and apply mixture to scalp with cotton wool. Use BEFORE shampooing.

To soothe tired eyes, put pads of cotton wool in a jar and cover with witch hazel. Leave in the fridge until needed. Place one pad on each eye and relax. Thin slices of cucumber may also be used.

To strengthen nails, soak fingertips in a cup of warm water containing a tablespoon of bicarbonate of soda. Dry and apply almond oil or handcream.

To soothe sunburn, mix half a cup of milk with a pinch of bicarbonate of soda and pat mixture gently over affected area. A little vinegar is also effective.

To minimize freckles, pat a little buttermilk on to your face and leave for ten minutes. Rinse off with cool water. This will help them to fade if you keep it up, but don't expect miracles.

A pleasant *skin tonic* is made up of 25 g (1 oz) liquid honey and 250 g (9 oz) of witch hazel or rose water. Mix well and use after cleansing. It refreshes the skin and prepares it for make-up and moisturizer.

Soak *nails* in a little warmed olive oil before a manicure to soften cuticles.

Rub the whole of *each foot* with warm olive oil once a week, massaging it in — excellent for prettier feet.

Brunettes: add a little vinegar to rinsing water when washing your hair. It gives burnished tones. *Blondes* can do the same with lemon juice, which helps to reduce oiliness too.

For dry hair, a trace of handcream (not lotion) rubbed on the palms of the hands and then lightly smoothed over the hair before brushing helps to counteract dryness and controls fly-away ends.

To economize on face powder, put a small quantity in the powder bowl and partially cover it with an appropriately sized disc of cardboard.

laundry and stains

A well-tried Welsh *washing tip for blankets*
which makes them mothproof at the same time:
3 dessertspoons of eucalyptus oil
1 large breakfast cup of methylated spirits
225 g (8 oz) best soap flakes.

Mix ingredients together in a screw-top jar until
all are dissolved, and keep until required.
Add one tablespoonful of the mixture to a gallon
of water and just soak blankets for washing in the
solution until clean. Then put them through the
wringer or spin dryer. DO NOT RINSE as the
eucalyptus oil replaces the natural oil in the
wool and allows the blankets to retain their
original look and feel. Dry outside on a windy
day, supporting carefully to keep their shape.
NB The smell from the eucalyptus does NOT
linger.

For stained feet of white socks, add a small
quantity of bicarbonate of soda to the washing
water.

Carbon tetrachloride, used sparingly, will remove
a black *scuff mark* from a light shoe.

To get *tea towels* really clean, plunge them *dry*
into boiling water in which you have brought a
detergent to a good froth. Leave the towels to

soak until the water is cold, wring them out and rinse well.

Odd nylon stockings boiled together merge in colour, and some at least should be able to be used as pairs.

No need to iron *nylon or terylene curtains* if you wash them this way. Fold them up neatly and soak first, then wash, keeping the article still in its fold. Don't crumple. Rinse in the same manner and drip dry.

When drying sheets, fold them into four when still wet and peg with three pegs to the line. This way the material will not drop out of shape and will be much easier to iron.

To dry candlewick bedspreads. Choose a windy day and hang them over the line with the fluffy side inside. The friction from the wind will bring up the pile beautifully.

When drying woollies on a line, thread a nylon stocking through the sleeves and fasten the pegs to this.

To clean an iron, sprinkle Vim on to a piece of newspaper placed on the ironing board and iron the dry Vim vigorously with the hot iron, drawing the iron to the edge of the board if necessary.

Starch marks on an iron may be removed by rubbing with a cake of soap while the iron is still warm. Polish off with a clean cloth.

To dampen clothes for ironing, place them in a large plastic bag and splash with water. Screw up the top of the bag and leave several hours. (Do not leave longer than 24 hours for fear of mildew, especially in warm weather.)

When the washing has been left and is *too dry for ironing*, place it in the fridge for five minutes or a little longer if necessary.

To remove shine from trousers or skirts, sponge the affected areas with a weak ammonia solution — one teaspoon per 6 dl (1 pint) of warm water. Then press until perfectly dry with a damp cloth and warm iron.

When cleaning suede, brush over with lemon juice, then steam for a few seconds. Brush with wire brush and the suede will come up like new.

Removing stains from washable fabrics

Blood. Soak in cold salted water. Change water till clear, then wash in the usual way. Soak old stains overnight in a cooled solution of biological washing powder, then wash in usual way.

Coffee, cocoa, tea. Soak in detergent, or in warm water adding one tablespoon of borax, or two tablespoons of household ammonia per 6 dl (1 pint). Remove any remaining grease with a solvent such as Thawpit and wash finally in detergent.

Fruit and beetroot stains. Speed is essential. Put the kettle on and remove garment at once. Place affected material in a deep bowl, and pour boiling water directly on to the stain from a height.

Grass. For cottons etc, sponge with neat methylated spirits, but for nylon and rayon use it diluted with an equal quantity of water. Glycerine, rubbed into the stain and left for an hour, is an alternative. Finish by washing as usual.

Ink.
1 Fountain pen ink: soak in milk, then wash out in the usual way.
2 Ballpoint pens, felt tips, etc: dissolve in neat methylated spirits and wash out in usual way.
3 Marking ink, indian inks: take to the cleaners as soon as possible.

Lead pencil marks can sometimes be removed with methylated spirits.

Lipstick. Remove as much as you can with a knife, then work in Vaseline or glycerine to loosen the stain. Then wash in usual way.

Nail varnish. Nail varnish remover may be used safely on all fabrics except rayon and tricel. NB Protect working surface as the spirit will damage paint and furniture.

Perspiration. Never delay as it can damage fabric. Can be treated by:
1 Soaking in one part of ammonia to three parts of water.
2 Sponging with white vinegar.
3 Soaking in a solution of detergent.
   Then wash as usual.

Rust and iron mould.
1 Rub with half a lemon dipped in salt if stain is not bad.
2 Use a proprietary rust remover (Moval).
3 'Dygon' also gives excellent results.

Tar on fabrics. Apply:
1 Eucalyptus oil.
2 Lighter fuel (i.e. Benzine), specially good for clothes that need dry cleaning.

3 Butter, to soften the tar.
4 Brasso.

Tea. Rub Fuller's earth, or dry salt, into the stain and then brush off.

in the kitchen

To loosen screw-top bottles or jars, either:
1 Tap round the metal top sharply at an angle, or
2 Heat lid under a running hot tap, to expand the metal, or
3 Wind rubber bands round the lid tightly in order to get a firm handgrip, or
4 Grip cap with a pair of nutcrackers.

To keep your *table silver polished*, mix 1 tablespoon of ammonia with 1 teaspoon of silver plate powder and 1 cup of water. Soak a cloth in this mixture and hang it up until quite dry. Then use it to dry your silver.

To clean forks, fill a jar with about twelve milk bottle tops and a tablespoon of cooking salt dissolved in hot water. Stand the forks briefly in the jar as you wash up.

Soak *egg spoons* in the water in which the eggs have been boiled in order to remove egg stains.

Keep a twist of nylon net or an old toothbrush in a jar of Goddard's *silver* dip – then there is always something to hand for *awkward shapes* that will not go into the jar.

To clean the insides of silver teapots or jugs, put a tablespoon of washing soda and a few silver milk bottle tops in the teapot. Fill with boiling water and leave to stand. Rinse out well, leave to drain and dry thoroughly.

For *stainless steel teapots*, put a tablespoon of washing soda and fill with boiling water. Leave to stand and clean out as above.

For *chrome or aluminium teapots* NEVER use washing soda inside or out. The inside may be cleaned with fine wirewool. Rinse, dry thoroughly and store in a dry place. NB Dampness causes chromium plate to peel.

Chrome may be polished with a little bicarbonate of soda on a damp cloth. Rinse and dry thoroughly.

Aluminium may be polished with dry table salt.

To avoid the *musty smell* in a little-used silver or *metal teapot*, dry the inside well and put in a piece of butter muslin and a couple of sugar lumps before putting the pot away.

Darkened *aluminium pans* can be cleaned by boiling up cream of tartar and water in them. Two teaspoons to 1.2 litres (2 pints) of water.

If you have a *stained saucepan*, cook rhubarb or apple peel in it and the stains will disappear.

A musty smell in the refrigerator? Never use a disinfectant, for it can flavour food for months. Just wash out the inside with a teaspoon of bicarbonate of soda dissolved in warm water. Rinse with clear water and dry.

Freshen up vacuum flasks after winter storage by placing two teaspoons of bicarbonate of soda in the empty flask and top up with nearly boiling water. Leave to stand overnight, empty and wash in soapy water, then rinse out several times in warm water. A couple of sugar lumps kept in the dry flask will keep it fresh when not in use.

To clean a vacuum flask and remove tea or coffee stains, crush an eggshell and put it inside with a little hot water. Insert stopper and shake hard for a few minutes. Rinse out with clean hot water.

To polish up your *stainless steel sink unit*, rub it well with a newspaper.

Handy storage. Save screw-top jars and screw the tops securely to the underside of a shelf. The jars are then suspended from under the shelf. Useful for sugar, dried fruit, etc, and also for nuts and bolts and the like in the workshop.

A hand hairdryer may be used as a speedy aid to *defrost a fridge* or deep-freeze.

Washing-up liquid diluted with water to half-strength is still effective and a good economy.

As you empty a tin or packet from the store cupboard, throw it into your shopping basket to give you *a useful reminder for the next shopping list.*

A cap of gingham or other cotton, with pinked edges and secured with a rubber band, will dress up *a pot of home-made jam* for a gift or a sale.

A useful *hotplate or slow cooking surface* can be made by placing a small firebrick over a low gas ring, or even on an exposed pilot as found on some gas cookers. The firebrick will absorb and retain the heat and behave like a miniature night storage heater to provide a sustained and economical source of heat.

Add one teaspoon of mustard powder to the washing-up water to get *the smell of fish off silver,* and add one teaspoonful of vinegar to remove it from china.

If you can't get rid of *a smell in a saucepan,* try boiling a little neat vinegar in it for a minute.

A Worcestershire sauce bottle is a useful container for gravy browning. The 'dropper' top is ideal for controlling the browning and the very messy drips. The top is easily prised off from the neck of the bottle for washing and refilling.

If you have a *lettuce* with the roots attached, stand it with roots in water and it will keep fresh for a week. Strip off leaves as required. (This works particularly well with a 'Webbs' lettuce.)

To keep cabbage or lettuce without a refrigerator either:
1 Wrap it in wet newspaper, or
2 Stand it in a bowl or bucket with a little water at the bottom and leave in a cool place, or
3 Place it in a saucepan, or other airtight container, with a tightly fitting lid.

Washed lettuce, watercress and parsley wrapped in a plastic bag may be kept for several days in the refrigerator. Lettuce stays crisp for serving in this way. Parsley can be kept for greater lengths of time in the freezer compartment.

To freshen lettuce, immerse it in a mixture of vinegar and water.

If *tomatoes* are a little soft and over-ripe, soak

them in salted water for about half an hour. They should become firm.

Before putting away tomatoes or any green vegetables, put a few tissues in with them to prevent them from becoming moist and to keep them firm for longer.

To keep *a half-used tin of tomato purée* fresh, pour a little cooking oil on it to cover the surface and put it in the fridge.

A slice of bread in a cake tin will *keep the cake moist*. When the bread dries out replace with a fresh slice.

To keep a *fruit cake moist*, put an eating apple into the tin when storing it.

To keep *biscuits crisp*, put a cube of sugar into the tin with them.

How often do you use a whole *Brillo pad* on one saucepan ? Cut them in half to save waste.

Wrap *Brillo pads* in tin foil to prevent rusting.

Make your own *saucepan cleaner* from a good collection of nylon net bags. Put one inside another and secure strongly with a piece of string.

To prevent *scouring powder* solidifying from steam, keep a tin lid on top of the holes.

Fit your packet of *washing powder* into a plastic bag and it will then be protected from wet hands and wet surfaces.

To clean decanters, or other small-mouthed glass containers, use half warm water, half vinegar and half a cup of sand. Shake hard and leave to stand. (Lead shot, when obtainable, can be used instead of sand with excellent results.)

Rub common salt on *teacups* to remove stains.

Use Milton to get rid of tea and coffee *stains on Melamine cups*.

Line the bottom of your oven with tinfoil to catch the drips that would otherwise burn. It can also be used underneath the boiling rings for the same purpose.

Avoid washing an *omelette pan* — wipe round it with clean kitchen paper after use.

Stained hands and fingers can be whitened by rubbing with the inside of half a squeezed lemon.

To get rid of *ants in the kitchen*, choose a proprietary brand of pet insecticide which will be safe for pets and humans.

To cook salmon to be eaten cold, plunge it into boiling water containing a little lemon juice, salt and pepper. Keep it on the boil for three minutes and leave it to cool in the liquid.

To cook sprats without frying, roll them in seasoned flour and then thread them on to metal skewers. Place in a greased meat tin and cook 20 minutes or so in a hot oven.

When grilling kippers, put a tablespoon or two of water under them and they will keep moist.

Sauces for fish
1 A quick sauce can be made by mixing some bottled sandwich or cucumber spread with a little bottled salad dressing and a spoonful or two of milk to thin. Heat gently (do not boil).
2 Alternatively, salad dressing can be thinned with milk, and chopped chives or spring onions added.
3 Try a little heated chutney for a tasty change.

When skinning fish, dip the fingers in water and then salt to grip the skin and prevent it slipping.

To coat meat, fish, etc with flour, place all ingredients in a bag or plastic box with a fitting lid and shake gently.

To make a crisp batter for frying fish or making fritters, add half to one teaspoonful of Birds Golden Raising Powder and beat well before using.

As an economical alternative to eggs when *coating fish for frying*, mix equal quantities of custard powder with flour.

A small quantity of custard powder mixed with milk may also be used when *brushing the top of pastry* and scones.

When roasting meat, place it on a meat-rack in the baking tin rather than on the bottom of the tin itself. This saves at least one portion of meat.

When you are about to pluck *game or poultry*, first immerse the bird in boiling water for about one minute. This makes plucking easier and avoids the problem of flying feathers.

Suet dumplings flavoured with your favourite herbs are a tasty 'filler' in a hotpot or stew.

Over-salted casseroles can be remedied by adding a few pieces of raw potato.

Quick porridge oats make a good *thickening for*

mince, and increase the bulk. The consistency is very similar. Use proportions of approximately two tablespoons of oats to 450 g (1 lb) of mince. Add gravy browning to give a good rich colour.

When making a pie which needs a funnel, get the butcher to give you a small marrow bone to use instead.

Add a handful of white breadcrumbs to 225 g (½ lb) of sausage meat when making *Scotch eggs* – it makes the sausage meat go much further.

Cold meat and fish will go further in *sandwiches* if put through the food mincer first. Moisten with butter or margarine if necessary.

When *egg yolks* are not wanted for immediate use, drop them into a basin of cold water and put them in a cool place : they will keep for days.

A simple way to *separate the yolk of an egg from the white* is to break the egg into a saucer, upturn a small glass over the yolk and pour off the white.

Place *hardboiled eggs* straight into cold water to prevent them becoming discoloured.

To peel hardboiled eggs easily, crack eggshell well by tapping on hard surface, slip in the end of a curved spoon or fork handle, and ease the shell off.

Add a small quantity of vinegar to the water when *boiling eggs* to prevent the white from leaking out.

Prick *eggs before boiling* to avoid cracking.

A simple method of *poaching an egg* is first to bring a pan of water to the boil, then turn off the heat and swirl the water round with a spoon. Break the egg into the swirling water, and cover closely with a lid. Leave for two minutes or so, when the egg will be nicely set. A teaspoon of vinegar and a pinch of salt should be added to the water.

Rub salt into a new, or washed, *frying pan* with some paper before using it – this will smooth the surface and promote a non-stick effect.

Scrambled egg will not stick to the saucepan so tenaciously if you first melt the butter and roll it well round the pan before adding the egg.

When making *scrambled eggs*, remove from heat when three parts cooked, cover and leave

the mixture to finish cooking in its own heat.
The egg will come away more cleanly, and the
saucepan will be easier to clean.

Chinese method of boiling rice
1 cup raw rice
2 cups, less 1 tablespoon, boiling water
1 level teaspoon salt

Bring it all to boiling point in a saucepan, cover
with a well-fitting lid and simmer for ten
minutes. Remove from heat, without removing
the lid or stirring, and keep in warm place for
another ten minutes. The rice will then be cooked
and the water absorbed. Fluff it up with a fork,
and if still too moist place a teatowel under the
saucepan lid, cover and put in a warm place.

If lemon juice is added to the water you are
boiling rice in, it will not only whiten, but also
separate the grains.

Fried rice. Fry raw rice in a little oil till the grains
are opaque and slightly toasted, then proceed
as for boiled rice (see above).

If you have a metal colander your *rice* can be
cooked very satisfactorily by *steaming* it in the
colander over a saucepan of water. It can also be
kept warm indefinitely by this method.

When boiling rice, peas or beans, rub round the top of the saucepan with a greasy paper or add a few drops of cooking oil to the water. The contents will not boil over so easily.

A teaspoon of oil added to *butter when frying* will help to stop it burning.

When frying bread, moisten it first with milk: it fries better and saves fat.

When frying chips throw in diced carrot or any other root vegetable of choice for variety and cook them all together.

Crispy roast potatoes. First bring to the boil in well-salted water, drain and sprinkle liberally with flour. Then put them into a hot pan in which the meat is roasting and continue as usual.

New potatoes that have been scraped can be kept without discoloration for several hours if they are covered in water to which a few tablespoons of milk have been added.

New potatoes. Soaking them for a few minutes in hot water to which a little bicarbonate of soda has been added helps to make them easy to scrape.

When peeling potatoes, place a colander in the bowl of water and peel the potatoes into it. When finished, lift the colander from the bowl complete with peelings.

When leaving peeled potatoes overnight, a slice of bread in the water will stop them becoming discoloured.

When cooking *baked potatoes*, push a metal skewer through each one from end to end. The potatoes will then cook in half the usual time: the skewer acts as a heat conductor.

To prevent the *smell of cooking cabbage* or cauliflower, squeeze a little lemon juice into the water.

To dry a quantity of *lettuce*, after washing put it in an old pillow case and give it a few seconds' spin in the spin dryer.

When making jam:
1 Clip a clothes peg on to the handle of the wooden spoon and lodge it over the edge of the pan to prevent the spoon falling in.
2 Add a knob of butter to boiling jam and it will help to prevent scum forming.
3 Allow jam to cool off for a few minutes, then

stir well before potting and 'scum' will disperse.

When potting hot jam, stand the warmed jars on a board or a newspaper. Use a small jug (warmed) to scoop out the jam, holding a saucer under it as you pour, to catch any drips.

For a rich golden brown *marmalade,* replace a tablespoon or two of white sugar with the same quantity of soft brown sugar.

The waxed paper from cereal packets is useful for making the waxed circles used for *sealing home-made jam.*

Jampots may be covered very simply without string or rubber bands by using a self-clinging plastic food wrap.

To keep *pancakes* soft, beat 25 g (1oz) or so of melted butter into the batter.

To prevent *baked custard* from separating out:
1 Heat milk to boiling point and allow to cool before adding other ingredients.
2 Stand in a pan of water in the oven to ensure slow cooking.

Ideal milk will whisk more easily if kept in the fridge for a few hours beforehand.

Peeled apples will not turn brown if you put them immediately into some moderately salted water, or water with a little lemon juice added, for five or ten minutes.

To skin grapes, tomatoes or oranges, plunge them into boiling water for two minutes, then into cold ; the skins will then come off without difficulty.

Grate or pare the *skins of oranges and lemons* before using the fruit, and store the skins in a carton in the freezer for flavouring cakes and puddings later.

When only a small amount of *lemon juice* is needed, make a hole in the lemon with a skewer, squeeze out the amount you need, then wrap the lemon in kitchen foil and keep in the fridge until required again.

To make *juice flow easily from oranges and lemons*, drop them in boiling water for a few minutes before squeezing.

Before *grating oranges and lemons*, dip the grater into cold water : the peel will slip off the grater.

Whipped cream will be lighter and much greater in volume if the whisked white of an egg is folded into it. (This is not suitable for piping.)

To set a jelly quickly:
1 Stand the mould in a basin of cold water, with the water level half-way up the mould. Add a handful of salt to the water.
2 Dissolve the cubes in a very little boiling water and make it up to the quantity required with ice-cubes, if available.
3 Put jelly into the ice-trays in the freezer compartment of your fridge and turn the dial to maximum coldness. (Useful when the jelly has to be chopped anyway, as it emerges in a rather odd shape.)

To store an *iced cake*, place it on the lid of the tin and invert the tin over the cake, so making it much easier to remove the cake for serving.

Sprinkle sugar on top of hot *boiled custard* to prevent a hard skin forming.

Dust scales with flour first when *weighing treacle* and it will flow off easily.

When boiling the *Christmas pudding*, place the basin on two skewers if you have no trivet, to ensure a good circulation of water.

Leave the *Christmas cake* mixture in its tin for 24 hours before baking and it will retain the moisture better.

Mix strong cold tea instead of beer or stout with *Christmas pudding* mixture — it will darken it and help keep it moist.

A bowl of water placed in the oven when the gas or electricity is turned on will help to keep a rich *fruit cake moist*.

If *angelica or cut candied peel* hardens and becomes tough, it can easily be softened by soaking in hot water for a few minutes.

A small quantity of glycerine added to *royal icing* prevents it becoming too brittle.

Walnuts soaked overnight in salty water can more easily be cracked without breaking the kernel.

To shell *Brazil nuts* easily, put into a saucepan of cold water, bring to the boil, boil one minute, then put into cold water. Drain and leave to dry thoroughly in a warm place.

The base of a *sponge cake* will be loosened from

the tin by placing tin on a damp cloth for a minute before turning out.

To make a simple *decoration on a sponge cake* put a doyley on top of the cake and dust it with icing sugar.

To bake blind *flan cases* use cooking foil and tuck well into corners. Remove 5 minutes before full cooking time.

Pastry is improved by being chilled in the fridge for 30 minutes before cooking – but remember to allow another 30 minutes for it to thaw out before rolling.

Shortcrust pastry mixture, before the water has been added, can be stored for up to 5 days in a jar in the fridge and this makes for a lighter pastry. It can also be stored in this way with added sugar and used as a crumble top.

When making *pastry*, keep a polythene bag beside you and slip your hand into it to pick up the phone, open the fridge, etc. This avoids making a mess.

When rubbing fat into flour, cool fat in the fridge until very hard and, using a coarse grater, proceed as usual. It saves time and gives a very light pastry.

Use *chopped dates* instead of dried fruit when baking. They taste delicious in scones or cakes and are cheaper.

Stale buns can be made delicious by dipping them in milk and heating them in a slow oven. Butter while hot.

If a *mixing bowl* moves around while you are mixing, place the bowl on a damp cloth and it will stay fast.

When opening a new *packet of marge*, cooking fat, etc, it is helpful to mark it off in 25 g (1 oz) divisions with a knife. Amounts can then be gauged without weighing after the packet has been started.

Keep a few marbles or pebbles in the bottom of your *double saucepan* — they will rattle when the water gets low and remind you to refill it.

Caramelize sugar in an old spoon if you are without *Bisto or gravy browning*.

A *toasted cheese sandwich* may be made by

first toasting the two pieces of bread on one side, laying slices of cheese between toasted sides, and finally toasting the resulting sandwich on both sides.

New bread may be cut into the thinnest slices by dipping the knife into boiling water before using.

To slice *tinned meat* much more easily, freeze first for an hour or so.

To prevent *boiling milk* from spilling over when you see it rising in the pan, remove from heat quickly and bump the saucepan sharply as you put it down.

To stop toast going soggy, tap each slice all over before putting in toast rack. This is known as 'kringling'.

Left-over white wine which has gone bitter may be added to vinegar.

Plastic shaped holders from chocolate boxes make lovely *novelty ice-cubes* for a party.

Add a little olive oil or cooking oil to loosen stiff *salad dressing*.

To chop parsley quickly put a few sprigs into a cup and snip up with the kitchen scissors.

Parsley sauce. Include parsley stalks finely chopped with the leaves for good flavour.

When making *mint sauce*, chop the mint and sugar together — this eases the task of chopping.

To keep *salt* free-running, keep a few grains of rice in the salt pot.

Fire on the cooking stove, or in the oven — sprinkle lavishly with salt or bicarbonate of soda to subdue flames and smoke.

Fun with flavours

To improve flavour and tenderness of *bacon or ham* add a tablespoon of *vinegar* and a teaspoon of *sugar* to the cooking water — when cooked leave it to cool in the liquor.

A tablespoon of *prune juice* added to soups etc, will enrich them.

A tablespoon of *vinegar added to a beef stew* will make the meat more tender, as well as making it taste good.

The *juice of an orange* and half the grated rind gives 450 g (1 lb) of *stewing steak* an unusual and delicious flavour. Add before cooking

Sift $\frac{1}{4}$ teaspoon *dry mustard* with each 225 g (8 oz) flour for *rich fruit cake* to develop mellow fruity flavour.

To enhance the taste of *strawberries*, place them in a dish, pour over the *juice of an orange*, and leave for a while before serving.

Mint sauce made with *lemon juice* is delicious for a change. Also try brown sugar – the flavour is very good.

Add a tablespoon of *peanut butter* to *fruit cake* mixture for a nutty taste.

Serve *tinned pineapple* with *roast chicken* or sausages. A sauce can be made by thickening the syrup with a little cornflour.

Cheese such as *Gruyère* is nicer cut very thinly. A potato peeler is good for this purpose. This idea is also useful when cutting cheese sandwiches.

A full-flavoured *seasoning* can be made and

stored as follows:

125 g (5 oz) salt
25 g (1 oz) white pepper
1 teaspoon cayenne pepper
1 dessertspoon ground mace
1 teaspoon celery salt
1 teaspoon caster sugar
½ teaspoon paprika pepper

Mix very thoroughly and store in an airtight jar.

Use about 1 teaspoon to 450 g (1 lb) of meat when stewing.

man about the house

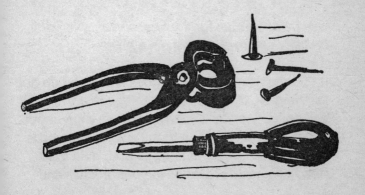

The use of a cellulose wallpaper paste painted over *old emulsion paint will help to remove it*. Leave for ten minutes before scraping.

To strip old wallpaper, damp it with warm water in which you have put a few drops of detergent washing-up liquid. This is as good as using an expensive stripper.

When pasting wallpaper, tie a piece of string across the top of the paste bucket, so making a useful ledge on which to rest the brush in between pasting. The same idea is useful when using a large can of paint – in order to rest the brush.

When soaking paint brushes in a jar, clip a clothes peg to the handle, and lodge over side of jar to keep the bristles off the bottom.

Use paint stripper for the final *cleaning of paint brushes* before putting them away.

If you require to *work near the ceiling* and do not like heights, try clamping or screwing a 5-cm by 2.5-cm (2-inch by 1-inch) piece of wood about 3 metres (10 feet) long to the side of your steps so that you have something to grab hold of to steady yourself. Tie loops to your brushes and tools and hang them on cuphooks screwed into this steadying rail. This will save a lot of clambering up and down the steps.

To cut down the smell of paint, cut an onion in two and put it cut sides up in the room while you are painting. Then throw it away.

If you wish *to fix wall lights* in an old room which once had gas lighting you may find that the use of the old gas pipes as conduits for your cables will save you a lot of chiselling and replastering.

A proprietary brand of paint stripper may be used *to remove lacquer* from (treated) brass ornaments.

To clean marble, paint the surface with a mixture of one part powdered pumice, one part powdered chalk and two parts bicarbonate of soda. Leave this on the marble for at least a day and then wash off with clean water and a soft nail brush or firm sponge. Shiny marble can be repolished by using whiting with a chamois leather. Do not use soap or detergents that could discolour the marble.

Grease spots on wallpaper. Place a piece of blotting paper on the wall and iron over it with a warm iron.

To locate screw holes for fixtures when repapering, place a matchstick in the rawlplug so that it protrudes about 3 mm ($\frac{1}{8}$ inch). When you brush down the new wallpaper the matchstick pops through the damp paper showing the exact position for the refixing of the screw.

If there is a danger of *plaster cracking* when driving a picture nail into the wall first stick a piece of sellotape over the plaster.

A simple *'pin up' area* can be made by sticking polystyrene ceiling tiles to the wall.

When planning the colour scheme for redecorating a room a useful guide is 75% main colour, 15% contrast and 10% 'splash'. Keep strong or dark colours at low level.

Use old pyjamas or shirts as *painting overalls*.

To prevent the wood splitting when nailing near the end of a piece of wood, first give a couple of hammer taps to the nail point. This slight blunting of the nail reduces the danger of splitting.

Tintacks are impossible to hold in corners between thumb and forefinger. Push the tack through a piece of thick paper or a piece of cigarette packet. By holding the paper you can position the tack without risk of bruised fingers or bent tacks.

Roughen the head of your *hammer* with emery paper in order to give a *better grip* to the head of the nail and avoid slipping.

When a chrome screw is needed use a steel screw of the same size to make a guiding hole into the rawlplug first. Rub the chrome screw with soap (not oil) to prevent rusting and screw it into place. NB Chrome screws easily bend or break.

When unscrewing tight screws, first of all turn the screwdriver slightly in the tightening direction and then immediately in the opposite direction. If the screw is rusty, a drop or two of vinegar or oil will sometimes help.

For *makeshift rawlplugs* use spent matchsticks.

Soap or candle grease rubbed on the bottom edges of a *stiff drawer* will make it run smoothly.

To saw a piece of wood with a straight and accurate cut. Score the wood with a Stanley knife run along a steel rule along the line to be cut. Then, holding the knife at an angle, make a second cut parallel to the first and a fraction away to the offcut side. This cut should pare out a tiny wedge of wood. The saw will follow the resulting channel, and will not jump or wander.

To prevent waste pipes from freezing up, keep basin and bath plugs in place, especially at night, and repair any dripping taps without delay.

Having released the screw from the *U bend of a waste pipe*, grease the thread with Vaseline before screwing up again. This makes it easier to undo the next time.

Dry rot can be treated by painting the affected wood with petrol. The fungus will turn black and die. NB If you smoke whilst carrying out this treatment you will probably also turn black and die !

Car washing. A soft-bristled handbrush dipped into the bucket of detergent will be found very useful for getting into awkward corners.

For *a good car wash*, use a bucket of hot water laced with paraffin oil. Allow to dry off on its own, and a polished surface will result.

When washing very *dirty hands* after car maintenance or other grimy jobs, take a generous squeeze of neat washing-up liquid or soft soap solution. Rub well into the skin and allow to dry for a few minutes before washing in the usual way. Rinse well and your hands will be clean.

'*Ring-pulls*' *from drink cans* are useful when nailed to the handles of light tools and brushes, etc, which can then be hung up on a wall out of the way.

To clean an oil painting, rub its surface with the flat side of an onion cut in half.

Having *defrosted* a domestic refrigerator, keep the *resulting water which, being distilled*, can be used in car radiators and batteries, and in steam irons.

Warning! *Fishy smell when there is no fish?* Could be plastic casing of electric appliance overheating. Turn off everything and send for an electrician.

pins and needles

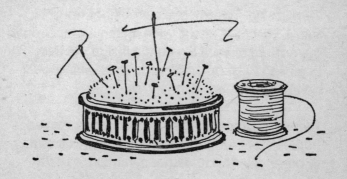

When using *double cotton*, put a knot in each end separately to prevent it getting tangled.

When *threading* machine or sewing needles place something white behind the eye of the needle.

For a bolder effect in *top stitching*, thread up the sewing machine with double thread – on the top only.

A pair of eyebrow tweezers prove excellent for *removing unwanted threads*, for example when taking out tacking, or re-sewing a button.

To prevent strain on a zip. When inserting, place the lower end about 6 mm ($\frac{1}{4}$ inch) below the end of the opening. Stitch across seam firmly by hand.

Turn-up tip. To protect a new pair of trousers, sew 1.25-cm ($\frac{1}{2}$-inch) wide matching tape round the bottom of each leg on the inside. As this begins to wear out, replace it, thus saving wear on the trouser legs themselves.

When pressing the hem of a garment, press edge firmly before turning up – then be very careful to press only this fold after hemming, so as to avoid the mark of the edge of the double thickness at the depth of the hem showing through.

When setting in a sleeve, the material will be eased with much less trouble if, keeping the right sides together, the work is held with the shoulder of the garment to the underside and the sleeve then resting on the top so that it can be eased to take the outside curve.

Shoulder straps can be kept in place by fixing a 3-cm (1½-inch) piece of ribbon to the shoulder seam with a snap fastener at the other end.

After sewing *buttons* on to a garment, paint the thread with colourless nail polish and they will stay on much longer. This is especially good for children's clothes which have to take a lot of wear.

To avoid sewing *buttons* on too tightly, separate them from the fabric with a hairgrip or matchstick.

When *pyjama trousers* wear thin, make the jacket short-sleeved and use the spare material for making patches.

An old shirt, worn back to front, makes a good painting *overall for a child*. Just shorten the sleeves, thread elastic at the cuff, smarten up with a front band, and fix tapes to tie at the back. Cut off tails and hem.

To repair a zip broken at the base pull down the slide below the fractured teeth and cut out the broken teeth. Then run slide above the gap, engaging the teeth on both sides. Stitch the zip together firmly just above the broken area.

A 12.5-cm (5-inch) zip sewn into an inside jacket pocket will keep the contents safe – particularly useful on children's clothes.

A very cheap, washable and springy *filling* for soft toys or cushions can be obtained by unravelling old, clean knitted garments. Do not bother to wind the wool into balls, just unravel it in a mass, then chop it up a bit with some sharp scissors. Old nylon stockings cut into small pieces can also be used.

When working a *long piece of knitting* or crochet, put a marker at regular intervals along the side edges. When sewing up, match the markets, so keeping the seam even.

When *knitting pockets* for a cardigan, cast on two more stitches for the lining than you cast off for the opening. Then, when knitting lining into the garment, knit two together at both ends of the join. This makes a firmer join and does not stretch as a single stitch would.

To repair a hole in a knitted garment, first proceed as in the first stage of normal darning. Then, starting from the left-hand corner, bring the needle up to the top sound stitch. Travelling down, complete a series of chain or lazy-daisy stitches, each time picking up a cross-strand. From the bottom of the hole, work the needle up to the top again as in ordinary darning. Continue this way until the hole is filled. In a plain knitted garment the repair should be almost invisible. Reinforce on the underside if necessary.

To prevent the *elbows wearing through* on your and your family's jumpers, sew on leather elbow pads, which are available at most haberdashery shops and departments.

Sew a strip of leather round the *hems of jeans* to prevent them fraying.

Salvage buttons and zips where possible from worn-out clothes, such as those left over from a jumble sale.

flowers and plants
in the house

To preserve cut flowers in water

Daffodils and other bulb flowers. Cut off the white stem ends and rinse away the sticky white substance which is exuded.

Lilies. Cut the stem ends at a slant and give them a long drink up to their necks in water. Anthers heavy with pollen can be nipped off to prevent staining the petals.

Poppies. Singe bottom of stem in a candle or gas lighter flame to carbonize.

Roses. Gently remove any damaged outer petals and strip off thorns from the stem. Split or crush the stem.

Tulips. To prevent the stems from curving, wrap the bunch tightly in wet newspaper and stand in 5 cm (2 inches) of water for an hour or longer. Then push a short pin through each stem just below the flower-head.

Woody stemmed flowers. Split or crush the bottoms and dip in hot water if wilting.

(Remember to top up containers with water daily and if possible remove arrangements from a warm room at night.)

To revive a wilting flower arrangement, snip off ends of stems and stand in a little boiling water for a few seconds. Give the flowers a long cold drink up to the neck in cold water for a few hours then rearrange them.

Unconventional containers help to make attractive flower arrangements.

Crumpled chicken wire, or Oasis, is useful for securing flower arrangements. Secure in place with sellotape.

To preserve flowers and foliage

Pick *delphiniums, larkspur, achillea and large African marigolds* when they are perfect (when just open and before they start to fade – or drop their petals). Hang in small bunches, in a dry, cool, dark place – upside down. These are the easiest flowers to dry, in the simplest way.

To preserve foliage, cut small sprays of beech, oak, sweet chestnut, laurel, etc. Pick the mature foliage, as the young leaves wither more easily. Crush about 2.5 cm (1 inch) of the stem and leave overnight or longer in water. Put one part glycerine and two parts hot water in a jam jar (or other container) and stand the branches in the solution until they have absorbed it all, or have changed colour. If moisture appears on the leaves, remove them from the solution.
This process usually takes from one to two weeks. Do not use foliage which has started to change to autumn colouring, as this will only wither.

Coloured foliage, leaves and bracken of all types can be *pressed* between sheets of newspaper and placed under rugs or carpets. Green bracken dries to a soft grey-green shade which is very attractive when fresh foliage is scarce.

Many *grasses and seed pods* — from garden and hedgerow — are well worth drying (in the same way as flowers).

It is well worth while *experimenting* with other types of flowers and foliage — you never know what treasures you will discover!

Magnolia leaves, which have become skeletonized through lying under the trees, can be washed and gently scraped, and wired on to stems. You can even bleach them if you wish.

Leaves treated with glycerine and water will take on a lighter shade when placed in sunlight or fairly bright daylight.

Look for any well-shaped branches (either bare or lichen covered). They make a lovely, simple design, needing very few flowers.

One last point: NEVER use too many dried flowers. The result can be the kind of arrangement which provokes the comment – 'I don't like dried flowers'; but used with care, lovely effects can be obtained.

House plants
To prevent greenfly attacking your house plants, bury a clove of garlic in the soil in which the plant is growing.

Coffee grounds, cold tea and tea leaves are all excellent for mixing with the earth in flowerpots – particularly good for ferns.

Water your kitchen plants with tea left over in the teapot.

When going on holiday, put an old towel in the bottom of the bath, soak the towel in water, and stand all your plants on the towel to absorb the moisture gradually.

Water *African violets* by standing the pot in a bowl of water for an hour or so to avoid rotting the stem. Keep the flowerpot on wet coarse sand or wet moss and avoid a dry atmosphere.

If a *rubber plant has outgrown* itself a new plant may be obtained, while it is still growing, by first removing the bark of the stem 15 to 20 cm

(6 to 9 inches) from the growing tip. Cover this portion of stem with a ball of moist sphagnum moss. Tie securely in position, and cover with polythene to make an airtight package. New roots will grow into the moss in a few weeks, then the 'new plant' may be cut free and potted up.

in the garden

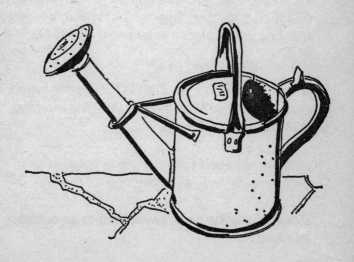

Broad beans sown in November escape the blackfly in the spring. When pods start to form pinch out the top of the plants. (These can be boiled to make a delicious vegetable.)

When 'sticking' runner bean plants, try crossing the sticks at about a third of the height from the ground. The beans themselves will then hang out vertically and can be seen easily for picking.

When watering runner beans or sweet peas in a drought, be sure to include the leaves and flowers. It is very important to keep the texture moisturized for proper development.

When planting outside tomatoes early, protect with heavy duty polythene fixed securely to long bamboo canes placed at an angle to a sheltering wall.

Roses do best in a position in the garden where they are shaded from the sun until the morning dew has dried off them.

Peace rose. Feed with manure in autumn and with fertilizer only at the second flowering.

When gathering roses always cut to an outside leaf bud.

Crushed eggshells under the seeds *when planting sweet peas* feed the plants with potash.

Pour boiling water on *parsley seed* before sowing to hasten germination.

Before planting peas and beans soak them for half an hour in paraffin ; this discourages mice. If possible roll them in red lead or flowers of sulphur.

Planting clematis. 'Head in the sun, feet in the shade'. Plant under existing tree and train up with a cane. It will grow up to the light and bloom over the top of the tree in a lovely shower. The 'feet' can also be kept cool by laying a flat stone over the base of the plant (or putting some low plant there).

Old nylons may be cut into *strips for tying up* in the garden.

Slug traps
1 Half an inverted grapefruit skin will trap slugs. Place slug pellets underneath the grapefruit.
2 Put a small tin in the ground with the top level with the soil, half full of milk and a little water. Slugs will crawl in and drown.

In a *herbaceous border staking* can be made less noticeable if twiggy branches are put round the plants in the spring. The plants then grow up through them, and are supported unobtrusively.

Empty plastic containers from yogurt, cream, etc, are useful for *cuttings and small plants*. Remember to pierce holes in the bottom when drainage is important.

Place *cuttings round the edge of a flowerpot* containing a dampened mixture of peat and sand. Stand the flowerpots (several at a time if necessary) in a large polythene bag and secure the top. No further attention is required. Inspect after a few weeks for root growth.

A handful of Epsom salts crystals sprinkled around the rhizomes of *irises* in the summer greatly improves the flowering the following year.

To encourage bushy growth, pinch out the top of a young plant.

The lilac tree should always be kept free of ground growth, and dead heads should be removed after flowering.

Do not remove dead heads of hydrangeas — they form valuable protection for next year's buds. Only prune them off when all danger of frost is past.

Treat your plants as you would a child — space to grow, not too much to eat and drink, but enough to sustain them. Warmth is important, especially when they are young, so shelter them with larger plants nearby, and when frosty cover them lightly with newspaper or straw as protection. Nature has her own balance so leave her to cope as much as possible.

Never take goodness from the soil without returning some. This need not become expensive — simply get into the habit of burying grass cuttings etc, and kitchen refuse in shallow trenches in your borders, or make a compost heap.

Take care not to use *grass mowings for a mulch* when the grass is seeding — or a good crop of weeds will result !

To prevent an *unpleasant smell from the compost heap* keep it watered in hot weather.

Wet newspaper is a good *substitute for compost* when planting roses, sweet peas or dahlias.

The right hand of a *gardening glove* wears out before the left ; turn a spare left-hand glove inside out to make another right-hand one.

An old hot water bottle filled with chopped foam rubber makes a good *kneeling pad*.

Old-fashioned straight potato peelers can be used *for digging weeds out of the lawn*.

Dogs' teeth are kept healthy and white by gnawing bones ; long or marrow bones are recommended — never rib or spinal bones, or chicken or fish.

Dogs' claws can be kept short by a reasonable amount of walking on pavements or hard surfaces.

Some dogs enjoy being vacuumed with the nozzle of a suction cleaner. Fine for moulting dogs and saves vacuuming everything else later.

An electric fan heater is useful for *drying long-haired* dogs. Introduce it slowly to avoid suspicion, and be careful to keep the heat moderate.

A dog shampoo (Kennels recipe)
1 part TCP
2 parts Stergene
3 parts water
Make up a convenient quantity and keep handy.

A very *young puppy* will be kept quiet and content in its basket if it has a *loudly ticking clock* for company.

Dog biscuits can be made from stale crusts,

preferably brown bread, cut in cubes, put on a tray at the bottom of the oven and baked until very hard. Cut-up pork rind, chicken skins, etc, baked with them will provide extra protein.

Rinse out the remains from all milk bottles and use as *a dog's drink*.

Grass is a natural 'medicine' to dogs, so allow them to follow their instinct.

Small birds are encouraged to your birdtray by crumbs rather than large pieces of bread. The crumbs from the 'rich man's' toaster are highly acceptable!

Kotina, or any other polystyrene, in a *cat's basket* will provide extra warmth.

A piece of damp foam rubber will help to remove *dogs' and cats' hairs* from upholstery and carpets.

Lingering and unpleasant smells in carpets or fabrics – spray with an Airfresh aerosol, and sponge with a cloth wrung out in hot water. Spray again, and if possible hang out in fresh air.

The back of a hand hung down loosely to be sniffed is often more acceptable to a *shy dog* than an outstretched palm.

Dog training classes are well worth attending with young dogs. They train you to train your dog and your future troubles will be halved.

Make 'hay' from your grass cuttings and store for rabbits and other pets. Crisp, dry leaves from the autumn also provide good bedding.

A solitary *caged bird* may pine and die. A 'friend' is easily provided by hanging a small mirror in the cage. Bells, swings and other toys are also welcome.

Layers of newspaper cut to shape is a perfectly satisfactory alternative to sanded paper for *caged birds*. When soiled, the top sheet can be easily folded over and removed.

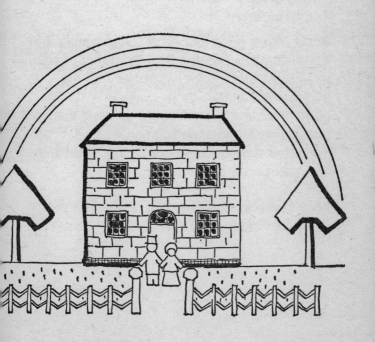

A good wedding cake

4 lb of love
1 lb butter of youth
½ lb of good looks
1 lb of sweet temper
1 lb of blindness of faults
1 lb of self forgetfulness
1 lb of pounded wit
1 lb of good humour
2 tablespoons of sweet argument
1 pint of rippling laughter
1 wine glass of common sense
1 oz of modesty

Put the love, good looks and sweet temper into a well-furnished house. Beat the butter of youth to a cream, and mix well together with the blindness of faults. Stir the pounded wit and good humour into the sweet argument, then add the rippling laughter and common sense. Work the whole together until everything is well mixed, and bake gently for ever.

Found in a church booklet of recipes printed at the turn of the century.

Marguerite Patten
Learning To Cook 70p

A book which tells you how to cook easily and economically, serve simple, appetizing meals, and know which foods should be at their best in each month of the year. The author gives advice on choosing kitchen equipment, filling the store cupboard, and what to do if things go wrong. There are suggestions for using up leftovers and ideas for parties, picnics and Christmas. Keep this book handy – and your family contented!

Mrs Beeton's All About Cookery £1.25

A new, completely up-to-date version of the cookery book world-famous for over one hundred years. Over 1,500 recipes cover every branch of cookery and in addition there are charts, lists, a glossary of kitchen terms and advice on choosing table wines.

'Designed to bring Mrs Beeton to the economic level of young housewives and mothers of larger families who have to watch their shopping allowance' THE EVENING NEWS

B.C.A. Turner
Pan Book of Winemaking 70p

This fascinating book describes in detail the history and methods of making delicious wines, ale and mead at a fraction of the retail price. Numerous recipes using a host of different fruits, vegetables and flowers are included as well as notes on wine clubs and competitions held annually all over Britain.

Catherine Fisher
The Pan Book of Dogs 80p
Now further fully revised by Muriel Fisher May

'A book that the tyro and the expert can read with pleasure and profit . . . seldom has a book of this kind provided so much wisdom for so little cash' COUNTRY LIFE

'One of the best bargains in years. Buying, feeding, grooming, training, caring, breeding, whelping, showing . . . everything is dealt with interestingly and thoroughly!' DOG WORLD

Rose Tenent
The Pan Book of Cats 70p

The complete guide to the cat: how to get your cat, what kind to have – long-haired or short-haired . . . Every breed is described, and we are told how to look after our cat – sick or well – how to show a champion cat, breed for profit and how to travel with a cat.

'From the pen of an acknowledged expert'
TIMES EDUCATIONAL SUPPLEMENT

'Clear and direct . . . painstakingly prepared, and we would recommend it strongly for any potential cat owner' OUR PETS